CW00394317

A
BOOK OF
BENEDICTIONS

By
Godfrey Holmes

MOORLEY'S Print & Publishing

British Library Cataloguing in Publication Data.
A catalogue record for this book is available
from the British Library.

Scripture quotations from the HOLY BIBLE,
NEW INTERNATIONAL VERSION,
copyright © 1973, 1978, 1984 by the International Bible Society

ISBN 0 86071 573 6

MOORLEY'S Print & Publishing
23 Park Rd., Ilkeston, Derbys DE7 5DA
Tel/Fax: (0115) 932 0643

Background cover photo courtesy Bigfoto.com

Dedicated to

the Memory of

Rev. ARTHUR JAMES HOLMES

He studied people's worship;

he took part in people's worship;

most weeks, he led people's worship.

At a set moment, the organ stopped playing.

Godfrey Holmes began to compile and compose prayers whilst still at Withernsea High School. More followed when, later, he taught Religious Studies in other schools.

His first book of prayers was
"BEGINNING WHERE I AM: Meditations for young people" published by S.P.C.K. Triangle.

"FREED FOR DEVOTION: A Carer's Book of Prayers" published by Moorleys is reviewed on page 55 of this book.

Godfrey Holmes' prayer specially written for B.B.C. Radio 4's DAILY SERVICE is:
> O God
> without whom nothing was
> that is –
> and nothing could be
> that has not been:
> mercifully grant that
> we appreciate all that is –
> and strive for all that could be.
>   Amen.

reproduced in: THE DAILY SERVICE PRAYER BOOK edited by Lavinia Byrne, and published by Hodder & Stoughton, 1998.

CONTENTS

5

To the God

who redeems us

when we feel beyond redemption;

who uplifts us

when we feel beyond retrieval;

who waits for us

beyond our furthest destination:

To that dependable God

be our unending devotion.

G.H.H.
2004

INTRODUCTION

When St. Paul wrote: "The Peace of God that passes all under-standing, keep your hearts and minds in the knowledge and love of Christ Jesus," he could hardly be aware he had formulated the most famous Benediction of all time, enriching, outgrowing, the small gathering of believers in Philippi to whom his letter was addressed.

To speak, speak well; to give, give thanks; to find peace, unfathomable peace: these are the essential ingredients of a Benediction.

Benedictions are beautiful - and Benedictions matter - because they are so often the Leader's closing words to the led. Hours or days later, the Benediction - its tone as much as its words - reverberate in the minds and memories of the faithful, and those who, having gone astray, wish to find their way back.

Blessings are everywhere, around and within. But with a formal blessing, a spoken Benediction, the leader is drawing attention to – indeed, drawing on - the grace of God:
- to guide people throughout their coming days,
- to comfort them in pain or distress,
- to strengthen the fainthearted,
- to assist those who have to make a decision,
- to befriend those who are lonely,
- to console those who are in mourning, and
- to gladden those who are saddened.

And these purposes are interchangeable. The person facing temptation might need comfort as well as resilience. The person who is forgotten might need tranquillity in addition to remembrance. Most of all, <u>everyone</u> needs the leader's blessing: "Till we meet again. . ."

People look forward to meeting again in the High Street, at the next meal table, at mid-week Bible Study. Yet for others - especially those travelling great distances - that "meeting again" could be months or years ahead. Many more people will interpret "meeting again" as meeting a loved one in Heaven, on another shore.

Benedictions are most powerfully used at funerals, committals, baptisms or weddings - where there is less chance that a congregation is familiar with communal worship.

The four key words of the traditional Benediction are NOW, MAY, LET and GO. Two handles: NOW and GO are active; two: MAY and LET are more passive.

Therein lies the simplicity of most Benedictions. Benedictions are not meant to be long or rambling; nor are they meant to be hurried; mere afterthoughts. The crafted Benediction links present and future. It closes one episode to open another, just as midnight December 31st closes one year to open another year of opportunity.

From Moses onwards, mystics have recognized that "mountain top" experiences have to be followed by a more humdrum existence [battle to survive?] in kitchen, office or shopping precinct. Many are those who wish to stay on the heights. And one such height – one such highlight - is the harmony of common worship, shared thanksgiving.

The Benediction does not begin: "Half-an-hour ago. . ." or "Tomorrow morning. . ." The leader's thoughts are far more immediate: *"NOW..."* without any further delay.

The Benediction continues: *"LET..."* - in other words, be open enough, be receptive enough, for the grace of God to come and make a difference, regardless of dilemma or obstacle.

Or else the Benediction introduces the notion of "MAY". The opposite of 'may' is 'may not', just as the opposite of might is might not. So when the leader announces: *"MAY..."* he or she urges the congregation not to create further problems, further barriers. Rushing water - better than a trickle - clears its own path. Gushing waters - better than meandering streams - have the power to effect change, to startle.

Finally, one of the most resounding words of both the Benediction and the concluding hymn is "GO!" or "GO FORTH!" Going is automatically the opposite of Coming. So an act of worship might start with the word "COME!" ["O Come all ye faithful!" "Come, ye thankful people, Come!"] - only to end with the instruction "GO".

Here again, this was something Adam, Noah, Moses, Aaron, Abraham, Amos, Isaiah and Jeremiah did long before John the Baptist, the Twelve - later the Seventy - Apostles. Going is not particularly easy unless one is going somewhere better. But at the actual moment of going, nerves jangle and apprehension fills the void.

The place one goes to is very likely to be less warm, less welcoming, less wonderful than where one already is.

Therefore *listen to* Benedictions, savour Benedictions, *remember* Benedictions, repeat Benedictions ... over and over again.

Also create Benedictions. They are some of the easiest of prayers to create - far easier, for instance, than Collects or Confessions. Usually one sentence, or one series of eventualities, is enough.

That is why, after collecting some Biblical Benedictions, and some last verses of hymns that act like Benedictions, I seek to create forty Benedictions of my own. Then I give pointers as to where readers can find yet other Benedictions: many handed down orally or in writing from generation to generation.

Exciting and engaging Benedictions are pivotal for future reflection, future action. They are - literally - an inspiration ... our reason to go forth; more important: to go forth with joy and confidence.

Without Benedictions, without blessings, we should be left in mid-air, awaiting a resolution, depending on our own resolve.

From the pulpit we hear:
    "The Grace of the Lord Jesus Christ, the Love of God, and
    the Fellowship of the Holy Spirit be upon YOU",
the congregation responding:
    "The Grace of the Lord Jesus Christ, the Love of God,
    and the Fellowship of the Holy Spirit be upon US".

Benedictions: benevolent, beneficial words - the ultimate **Feel-Good** Factor.

G.H.H.
March, 2004

DEFINITION OF THE BENEDICTION

AN ARROW PRAYER
A short, pointed utterance or aspiration, definitely only one sentence in length. May or may not be a Benediction.

A BENEDICTION
An act of blessing; invoking a blessing; a grace.

In this collection, "Benediction" is the term consistently used for something that sounds like a Benediction.

A BLESSING
Wishing goodness and happiness on behalf of self or God.

A CLOSING SENTENCE
By definition, a single sentence ending an act of worship.

A COLLECT
A *collecting together* of certain thoughts in a set pattern: a *SINGLE SENTENCE* including
i) Addressing God; ii) A relative clause; iii) The actual petition;
iv) The purpose of that petition; and v) An ending.

Collects are set for each Sunday and each Holy Day of the year, but there are thousands of other beautiful Collects quoted or collected elsewhere. Several Collects can also act as Benedictions - but in this book I have tried to use only one or two, most notably the Night Collect of the Church of England.

A COMMENDATION
A sentence or verse commending self, others, or congregation into God's care and keeping - especially applicable at the end of the day. Based on Jesus' words on the Cross: "Into Thy hands I commend my spirit." (A.V.)

A COMMITTAL
Different from stating a "commitment".
Usually a very specific prayer or sentence at a funeral, more so: a cremation, committing a body or a well-spent life to God's keeping throughout Eternity.

A DEDICATION
For the purpose of pronouncing a Benediction, a Dedication is a statement of intent to God that life, soul and future will be offered for that higher purpose.

A DOXOLOGY
A sentence or blessing or verse in praise of the Trinity: God the Father, Son, and Holy Ghost. May or may not be included in a Benediction.

AN EPILOGUE
A prayer or a total act of worship (usually brief) to close another related activity, like a youth club, a concert, or a communal meal.

A GRACE
A single sentence or verse giving thanks for a meal still to be eaten, or a special occasion still to be enjoyed - or conceivably, in both cases, a sentence or verse of ending.

A PETITION
Any request to God on behalf of self or others. Not all Benedictions contain a petition.

A RESPONSERY
The ending, or component, of an act of worship where the congregation replies to a Sentence or Psalm:

eg. Leader: "Go forth into the world in Peace."
      Response: "The God of Peace go with us."

A YIELDING
The act of offering self, soul, time, talent, to God.

BENEDICTIONS FROM THE BIBLE

The Lord bless you and keep you;
The Lord make His face to shine upon you
and be gracious to you;
The Lord lift up His countenance upon you,
and give you peace.

(Numbers 6)

Praise be to the name of God
for ever and ever -
wisdom and power are His.

(Daniel 2)

The Lord will watch over
your coming and going
both now and for ever.

(Psalm 121)

Praise be to the Lord God -
who alone does marvellous deeds.
Praise be His glorious name for ever;
may the whole Earth be filled with His glory!

(Psalm 72)

May God Himself, the God of peace,
sanctify you through and through.
May your whole spirit, soul and body
be kept blameless at the coming of our Lord Jesus Christ.

(1 Thessalonians 5)

To Him who loves us
and has freed us from our sins by His blood
and made us to be a kingdom
and priests to serve His God and Father -
to Him be glory and power for ever and ever.

(Revelation 1)

To Him who sits on the throne
and to the Lamb
be praise and honour and glory and might
for ever and ever!

(Revelation 5)

Salvation belongs to our God
who sits on the throne.
Praise and glory and wisdom and thanks
and honour and power and strength
be to our God for ever and ever! Amen.

(Revelation 7)

These then are the things you should teach;
Encourage and rebuke with all authority.
Do not let anyone despise you.

(Titus 2)

Never be lacking in zeal;
but keep your spiritual fervour,
serving the Lord.

(Romans 12)

Grace, mercy and peace
from God the Father and Christ Jesus our Lord.

(1 Timothy 1)

Therefore go and make disciples of all nations,
baptizing them in the name of the Father
and of the Son and of the Holy Spirit,
teaching them to obey everything I have commanded you.
And surely, I am with you always,
to the very end of the age.

(Matthew 28)

Forgetting what lies behind,
and straining forward to what lies ahead ...
press on towards the goal to win the prize
for which God has called us heavenwards.

(Philippians 3)

The peace of God,
which trancends all understanding,
will guard your hearts and your minds in Christ Jesus.

(Philippians 4)

May the grace of the Lord Jesus Christ
and the love of God,
and the fellowship of the Holy Spirit
be with you all.

(2 Corinthians 13)

The God of peace, who through the
blood of the eternal covenant brought
back from the dead our Lord Jesus,
that great Shepherd of the sheep,
equip you with everything good
for doing His will,
and may he work in us what is pleasing
to Him, through Jesus Christ,
to whom be glory for ever and ever. Amen.

(Hebrews 13)

15

Now to Him who is able to do
immeasurably more than
all we ask or imagine,
according to His power
at work within us:
to Him be glory in the Church,
and in Christ Jesus
throughout all generations.

(Ephesians 3)

To Him who is able to keep you from falling -
and present you before His glorious
presence without fault, and with great joy;
to the only God, our Saviour,
be glory, majesty, power and authority,
through Jesus Christ our Lord,
before all ages and now and for ever.

(Jude)

Oh the depth of the riches of the
   wisdom and knowledge of God!
How unsearchable His judgments,
   and His paths beyond tracing out!
Who has knowledge of the mind of the Lord?
   Or who has been his counsellor?
Who has ever given to God,
   that God should repay him?
For from Him and through Him and to Him
   are all things.
To Him be glory for ever!

(Romans 11)

Now to the King eternal, immortal, invisible, the only God:
be honour and glory for ever and ever.

(1 Timothy 1)

HYMN VERSES
USED AS BENEDICTIONS

Single verses from hymns and songs make excellent blessings, doxologies and Benedictions.

Even so, they need selecting with care in order that they end a particular gathering on the right note - nothing florid.

The following are simply a few of my favourites. There are hundreds of others: not necessarily the *last* verse of a particular hymn or song.

Words have had to be slightly adapted to the plural form - but it remains my belief that *wholesale adaptation* to make hymns sound "modern" destroys their rhythm and their impact.

> Forth in Thy name, O Lord, we go:
> Our daily labours to pursue.
> Thee, only Thee, resolved to know
> In all we think or speak or do.
> *(Charles Wesley, 1707-98)*

> All that we are or have:
> Thy gifts so free,
> In joy, in grief, through life,
> O Lord for Thee.
> And when Thy face we see,
> Our ransomed souls shall be,
> Through all eternity:
> Something for Thee.
> *(Sylvanus Phelps, 1816-95)*

Not disobedient to Thy heavenly vision.
Faithful in all things, seeking not reward.
Then, following Thee, may we fulfil our mission:
True to ourselves, our brethren, and our Lord.

(William Jenkins, 1868-1920)

Here then to Thee Thy own we leave:
Mould as Thou wilt the passive clay;
But let us all Thy stamp receive,
But let us all Thy will obey:
Serve with a single heart and eye,
And to Thy glory live and die.

(Charles Wesley, 1707-88)

Lord, in the strength of grace -
With a glad heart and free,
Ourselves, our residue of days:
We consecrate to Thee.

(Charles Wesley, 1707-88)

In a service which Thy will appoints
There are no bonds for me:
For my inmost soul is taught the truth
That makes Thy children free:
And a life of self-renouncing love
Is a life of liberty.

(Anna Waring, 1820-1910)

Green pastures are before us
Which yet we have not seen;
Bright skies will soon be o'er us
Where the dark clouds have been.
Our hope we cannot measure,
Our path to life is free;
Our Saviour has the treasure
And we will walk with Thee.

(Anna Waring, 1820-1910)

We faintly hear, we dimly see,
In differing phrase we pray;
But dim, or clear, we own in Thee
The Light, the Truth, the Way.
(John Greenleaf Whittier, 1807-1892)

Let us then with gladsome mind
Praise the Lord, for her is kind:
For His mercies aye endure,
Ever faithful, ever sure.
(John Milton, 1608-1674)

All praise and thanks to God
The Father now be given.
The Son, and Him who reigns
With them in highest heaven:
The one, eternal God,
Whom earth and heaven adore;
For thus it was, is now,
And shall be evermore.
(Martin Rinkart, 1586-1649)

Thine for ever! Thou our guide,
All our wants by Thee supplied,
All our sins by Thee forgiven:
Lead us, Lord, from earth to heaven.
(Mary Maude, 1819-1913)

Lead us, O Father, to Thy heavenly rest,
However rough and steep the path may be:
Through joy or sorrow, as Thou deemest best,
Until our lives are perfected in Thee.
(William Burleigh, 1812-1871)

O that each in the day
Of His coming may say:
We have fought our way through.
We have finished the work
Thou didst give us to do.

(Charles Wesley, 1707-1788)

Lord, we Thy presence seek;
May ours this blessing be;
Give us a pure and lowly heart,
A temple fit for Thee.

(William Hall, 1793-1861)

Now the day is over:
night is drawing nigh
Shadows of the evening
steal across the sky.
When the morning wakens:
then may we arise –
Pure and fresh and sinless in Thy holy eyes.

(Sabine Baring-Gould, 1834-1924)

If on our daily round, our mind
be set to hallow all we find,
New treasures still of countless price,
God will provide for sacrifice.

(John Keble, 1792-1866)

Father Divine, we come to Thee,
We yield as captives to Thy sway,
That love's gold chains may set us free
For all the burden of the day.

(George Mathieson, 1842-1906)

Direct, control, suggest, this day:
All we design, or do, or say
That all our powers, with all their might,
In Thy sole glory may unite.
(Thomas Ken, 1637-1711)

Grant us Thy peace upon our homeward way:
With Thee begun, with Thee shall end the day.
Guard Thou the lips from sin, the hearts from shame
That in this place have called upon Thy name.
(John Ellerton, 1826-93)

Go with us, Lord, from hence; we only ask
That Thou be sharer in our daily task.
So, side by side with Thee,
shall each one know
The blessedness of heaven begun below.
(William Jenkins, 1868-1920)

೮೦೮೦೮೦೮೦೮೦

We are so used to hearing the following doxology that it is hard to remember it is also the verse of a metrical hymn for worship: not one hymn, but *twin* hymns - Bishop Ken's perfectly balanced hymns for each morning and each evening.

Many other hymn-writers had a format for drawing all their previous verses together, but nothing to match this exactly:

Praise God, from whom all blessings flow;
Praise Him, all creatures here below;
Praise Him above, ye heavenly host;
Praise Father, Son, and Holy Ghost.
(Thomas Ken, 1637-1711)

೮೦೮೦೮೦೮೦೮೦

There is a green hill far away.
FAR AWAY
There is an opportunity far away.
STILL FAR AWAY
There is reconcilliation far away.
FAR AWAY
There is a holiday far away.
STILL FAR AWAY
There is a clearing far away.
FAR AWAY
And our reunion is far away.
STILL FAR AWAY

O God,
now bring that green hill,
that opportunity, that reconcilliation,
that holiday, that clearing,
that reunion
much nearer:
much nearer than we could
ever imagine it to be.
MUCH NEARER
Thank you, God.

G.H.H.
2004

NEW BENEDICTIONS

I have written these 40 "new" Benedictions to four formulae:

I)	Ten Benedictions asking:	"May...."
II)	Ten Benedictions asking:	"Let...."
III)	Ten Benedictions stating:	"Now...."
IV)	Ten Benedictions invoking:	"Blessings..."

There are, of course, many other ways to start a Benediction, but *cleverness* should never be the foundation for any Prayer ... or else the pray-er will be found out, undermined, ignored.

Because of the way mind and memory work, I might well have drawn unconsciously on existing Benedictions in church, in chapel, on radio, on the printed page. If that is the case, and the reader feels he or she owns those words put in that particular way, my sincere apologies.

MAY......

May Christ the Guiding Light
shine on the pathway that is this coming week;
So, following that guidance,
we shall leave the darkness of confusion far behind us.

May our errors be speedily forgotten;
our accomplishments readily remembered.

May the same Jesus
who taught His close disciples
on a deserted hillside,
teach us – distant disciples
though we are -
on a crowded roadside.

May the God of wind and weather stay with us
when the winds of adversity blow against our intentions,
and when bleak weather would destroy our achievements.

May we never, going out from here,
live only in anticipation of the time we shall return.

May holy moments come to us
spontaneously this week,
banishing unholy moments
to a Wilderness
we would leave far behind us.

May all our prayers and petitions, today
and henceforth, be to the fulfilment
of your purposes in us, and through us.

May humility be our preference over boastfulness,
sanctity our preference over sinfulness -
now and always.

May our feet be swift to explore new avenues,
new drives, new pathways ...
until all our roads join in Heaven.

May trust be in our hearts and minds this coming week:
trust in our families, trust in our friends,
trust in our higher instincts ...
trust born of these sacred precincts.

ഇരു ഇരു ഇരു ഇരു

LET......

Let all our certainties be proclaimed,
All our uncertainties, reclaimed.

Let each family, this week,
find comfort and joy
in each other's company. Amen.

Let our faith, hope, and generosity
be our witness this year and always.

Let all we ponder, enact, or say, before nightfall,
be to your honour and glory. Amen.

Let our best expectations be enjoyed,
Our worst expectations endured,
now and in all the days that shall follow.

Let every day of this week be a holy day,
every night of this week: a holy night. Amen.

Let the wondrous presence of God
we have known here,
relieve all people troubled by guilt
or pain or sadness -
until all suffering shall cease,
one day of gladness.

Let our homes be as welcoming
as our churches [schools],
and our churches [schools]
as welcoming as our homes

Let each meal of this coming day [week]
be taken as a memory of Christ's Passion -
and never without our Thanksgiving.

Let each struggling, swerving, sinking, ship –
this night - reach its harbour safely. Amen.

ଅଅଅଅଅଅଅଅ

NOW ...

Now shall every window in our lives be clear,
Every door to our hearts: wide open.

Now may each candle lit –
or yet, unlit –
flicker to your honour and satisfaction.

Now we see stained glass inside, looking out.
In the coming week be our Direction
when we see that same glass outside, looking in.

Now give us that assurance:
We shall not suffer more than we can bear;
We may not prosper more than we can share.

Now we are in the company of people we know and love.
Bless us as we leave into the company
of those we shall not know -
those it might be difficult to love.

Now we are filled with many words of inspiration.
In forthcoming days, make us remember them afresh.

Now our thoughts turn to there, not here -
Yet here we would seek to understand out there,
whatever joys, whatever mysteries, whatever hardships,
we shall encounter in our partings.

Now the Cross on the altar, seen,
alters the dross in our lives, unseen.

Now there is the sound of a distant bell,
calling us to new territory, new opportunity,
some new responsibility.
When we cannot turn back, may we go boldly forward -
in your strength; and to your glory.

ଚୈଓ୍ଚଓ୍ଚଓ୍ଚଓ୍

BLESSINGS......

Blessings fall upon us
As water from a cascading torrent.

Blessings fill our vessels to the brim –
Never counting all that runneth over.

Blessings in access;
Blessings in process;
Blessings in success;
Blessings in recess.

Blessings in the early morning dew;
Blessings in the penetrating fog;
Blessings in the bright sunshine
Blessings in the darkest cloudburst.

Blessings coming on days we were unprepared for them;
Blessings coming in hours we had no time for them.

Blessings as the storm clouds gather;
Blessings when the storm clouds are above us;
Blessings as the storm clouds disperse.

Blessings in the kitchen;
Blessings in the classroom;
Blessings in the office;
Blessings in the bus depot;
Blessings in the service station;
Blessings in the workshop;
Blessings in the factory;
Blessings in each home of rest.

Blessings shall come that each of us will not see as blessings;
Testings shall come that each of us will not see as testings -
Yet you, God Almighty,
own each blessing, each testing - to our eventual benefit.

Amen.

Blessings of seed to stalk,
bud to blossom,
stem to bouquet:
be given to us, by us, from us, each day,
as we seek to do your perfect will.

Blessings flowing like a clear stream
through our daily lives:
cleanse us, nourish us, replenish us, sanctify us,
to-day and always.

Amen.

ಬಡಚಡಬಡಚಡಬಡಚಡ

It remains a wonderful challenge to make up blessings and Benedictions - but these should always aim to be fairly simple and kind to the ear. Sentences - and more so, verses - must not be trite or empty, treacly or merely epigrammatic.

ANCIENT BENEDICTIONS

May God, the Lord, bless you with all good
and keep you from all evil;
may He give light to your heart with loving wisdom,
and be gracious to you with eternal knowledge;
may He lift up His loving countenance
upon you for eternal peace.

(Dead Sea Scrolls)

The Lord Jesus Christ
be near to defend you,
within to refresh you,
around to preserve you,
behind to justify you,
above to bless you ...
who lives and reigns with
the Father and the Holy Spirit,
God for evermore.

(Anon, 10th.Century, adapted)

O Jesus ever with us stay;
Make all our moments calm and bright;
Chase the dark night of sin away;
Shed o'er the world Thine own true light.

(A Prayer of St Bernard, also sung as a hymn)

From the unreal lead me to the real;
From darkness lead me to light;
From death lead me to deathlessness.

(Ancient Indian Prayer)

May the road rise to meet you.
May the wind be always at your back.
May the sun shine warm on your face.
May the rains fall softly upon your fields.
Until we meet again:
May God hold you in the hollow of His hand.

("The Irish Blessing" trad.)

May the eternal God bless and keep us,
guard our bodies, save our souls, direct our thoughts,
and bring us safely to the heavenly country:
our eternal home -
where Father, Son and Holy Spirit ever reign,
one God for ever and ever.

(Sarum Breviary)

May God, the Lord, bless us with all heavenly benediction,
and make us pure and holy in his sight.
May the riches of His glory abound in us.
May He instruct us with the word of truth,
inform us with the Gospel of salvation,
and enrich us with His love,
Through Jesus Christ, our Lord.

(Gelasian Sacramentary)

God be in my head – and in my understanding.
God be in mine eyes – and in my looking.
God be in my mouth - and in my speaking.
God be in my heart - and in my thinking.
God be at mine end - and at my departing.

(Sarum Primer, 1527)

May God the Father bless us;
May Christ take care of us;
the Holy Ghost enlighten us
all the days of our life.
The Lord be our defender and keeper of body and soul,
both now and for ever, to the ages of ages.

(Aedelwald,
a 9th Century Saxon Bishop)

Christ be with me; Christ within me;
Christ behind me; Christ before me;
Christ beside me; Christ to win me;
Christ to comfort and restore me;
Christ beneath me; Christ above me;
Christ in quiet; Christ in danger;
Christ in hearts of all who love me;
Christ in mouth of friend and stranger.

(St. Patrick's Breastplate, second stanza)

May the grace of the Lord Jesus
Sanctify us and keep us from all evil;
May he drive far from us all hurtful things,
And purify both our souls and bodies;
May He bind us to Himself by the bond of love,
And may His peace abound in our hearts.

(Gregorian Sacramentary)

Deep peace of the running wave to you
Deep peace of the flowing air to you
Deep peace of the quiet earth to you
Deep peace of the shining stars to you
Deep peace of the Son of peace to you.

Ancient Scottish prayer
most associated with the Iona Community)

Remember, O Lord, what Thou hast wrought in us,
and not what we deserve;
and as Thou hast called us to Thy service,
make us worthy of our calling;
through Jesus Christ our Lord.

(Leonine Sacramentary)

Thine is the day, O Lord, and Thine is the night.
Grant that the Sun of Righteousness
may abide in our hearts,
to drive away the darkness of evil thoughts.

(Gelasian Sacramentary)

Incline mercifully Thine ear, O Lord,
to these our prayers, and fill our hearts
with Thy grace, that loving Thee
with unfeigned love
we may evermore be defended under
Thy most gracious protection,
and be accepted in all our prayers and services,
through Jesus Christ our Lord.   Amen

*(Ancient Collect found in
A Chain of Prayer Across the Ages, 1913)*

Watch Thou, dear Lord, with those who wake,
or watch, or weep tonight,
and give Thine angels charge over those who sleep.
Tend Thy sick ones; Rest Thy weary ones;
Bless Thy dying ones; Soothe Thy suffering ones.
Pity Thine afflicted ones; Shield Thy joyous ones;
And all, for Thy Love's sake. Amen

(St Augustine, 354-430)

BENEDICTIONS
FROM VARIOUS SOURCES

To God the Father, who first loved us,
and made us accepted in the Beloved:
To God the Son, who loved us,
and washed us from our sins:
To God the Holy Ghost,
who sheds the love of God
abroad in our hearts.
Be all love and all glory
For time and for eternity.

(Thomas Ken, 1637 - 1711)

Blessing and honour and thanksgiving and praise
more than we can utter, more than we can conceive,
be unto You, O holy and glorious Trinity:
Father, Son and Holy Ghost,
by all angels, all men, all creatures, for ever and ever.

(Thomas Ken, 1637 - 1711)

The circle of Jesus keep you from sorrow
The circle of Jesus today and tomorrow
The circle of Jesus your foes confound
The circle of Jesus your life surround

(David Adam, modern but in the Celtic tradition)

The hands of the Father uphold you
The hands of the Saviour enfold you
The hands of the Spirit surround you

(David Adam)

The weaving of peace be thine
Peace around thy soul entwine
Peace of the Father flowing free
Peace of the Son sitting over thee
Peace of the Spirit for thee and me
Peace of the one
Peace of the Three
A weaving of peace be upon thee.

Around thee twine the Three
The One the Trinity
The Father bind his love
The Son tie his salvation
The Spirit wrap his power
Make you a new creation
Around thee twine the Three
The encircling of the Trinity.
(David Adam, modern but in the Celtic tradition)

The joy to this day be yours
The joy of this week be yours
The joy of this year be yours
The joy of the Father be yours
The joy of the Spirit be yours
The joy of the Son be yours
Joy for ever and ever be yours.
(David Adam)

The Father on you His blessing bestow
The Son His love towards you flow
The Spirit His presence to you show
On you and all the folk you know
On you and all who around you go
The Threefold blessing may you know.
(David Adam, modern but in the Celtic tradition)

God's blessing be thine - and well may it spring;
The blessing divine; in thine everything.

(G.R.D. McLean's translation from Gaelic)

The eye of God with thee to dwell;
The foot of Christ to guide thee well;
The Spirit's pouring shower to swell
Thy rich and gen'rous fountain-well.

(tr. by G.R.D. McLean)

Yours be the blessing of God and the Lord -
The perfect Spirit His blessing afford.
The Trinity's blessing on you outpoured -
With gentle and gen'rous shedding abroad,
So gently gen'rously for you unstored.

(tr. by G.R.D. McLean)

May the Father everlasting
Himself take you, round you casting,
His own gen'rous arm engrasping,
His own gen'rous hand enclasping.

(tr. by G.R.D. McLean)

God of the elements,
    glory to thee
For the lantern-guide
    of the ocean wide;
On my rudder's helm
    may thine own hand be
And thy love abaft
    on the heaving sea.

*(Chosen for the cover of
G.R.D. McLean's Gaelic poems)*

The same blessings we crave
for our friends, relations, and acquaintances:
that we may all live in perfect love and peace together,
and rejoice together at the great day of the Lord Jesus -
in whose holy words we sum up all our wants.

(John Wesley, 1703 - 1791)

Lord Jesus Christ,
help us to follow more closely in your footsteps;
that we may manifest in our own lives
the compassion and understanding
you have shown in yours.

(Frank Colquhoun)

Into your hands I put myself:
that both in light and darkness,
You may work your good purpose.

(Richard Harries)

Christ our Saviour come to dwell within us,
that we may go forth
with the light of your hope in our eyes
and your faith and love in our hearts.

(Worship Materials)

Go forth into the world in peace;
Be of good courage;
Hold fast that which is good;
Render to no one evil for evil;
Strengthen the faint-hearted ;
Support the weak;
Help the afflicted;
Honour all people;
Love and serve the Lord,
rejoicing in the power of the Holy Spirit.

(The Revised Prayer Book, 1928)

May God in the plenitude of his love
pour upon you the torrents of his grace,
bless you and keep you for a happy eternity,
and receive you at last into immortal glory.
(Blessing used at the Consecration of Coventry Cathedral)

The blessing of the Lord
rest and remain upon all his people,
in every land, of every tongue;
the Lord meet in mercy all that seek him;
the Lord comfort all who suffer and mourn;
the Lord hasten his coming,
and give us, his people, the blessing of peace.
(Handley Moule, 1841-1920)

We commend unto you, O Lord,
our souls and our bodies,
our minds and our thoughts,
our prayers and our hopes,
our health and our work,
our life and our death,
our parents and brothers and sisters,
our benefactors and friends,
our neighbours, our countrymen,
and all believing people:
to-day and always.

(Lancelot Andrews, adapted)

Lord dismiss us with thy blessing -
that we, inspired by this hour,
may radiate light and life.   Amen

*(A Prayer based on
John Fawcett's hymn
with the same first line, C19)*

May the Baby of Bethlehem,
the Carpenter of Nazareth,
the Teacher of Galilee,
the Healer of Judea,
the Sufferer of Gethsemane,
the Prisoner of Jerusalem,
the Saviour of Calvary,
the Risen Lord of Emmaus,
and the Ascended Lord in Heaven -
Come to meet us on our journey.

*(Loosley adapted from an original
prayer by Bertha C. Krall)*

Grant, O Lord,
that what we have said with our lips,
we may believe in our hearts
and practise in our lives -
and of your mercy keep us faithful unto the end,
for Christ's sake.

(Revd John Hunter, early C20)

May the blessing of God Almighty
rest upon us and upon all our work
and worship done in his name.
May he give us light to guide us,
courage to support us,
and love to unite us,
now and evermore.

(A Chain of Prayer Across the Ages, 1913)

Bless all those that watch over our souls;
succeed their labours,
and give us grace to follow their godly admonitions.

(John Wesley, 1703 - 1791)

The Lord, the God of grace,
go with you, fulfil all your need,
and direct you in your ways to his glory,
this day and always.

(Used, mid C20)

Now may God whom we have worshipped
assure us of his Spirit for daily living -
through the grace of his eternal Son.

(Used, mid C20)

Now God who has loved us, and given us everlasting
consolation and good hope through grace :
comfort your hearts,
and establish you in every good word and work.

(A Chain of Prayer Across the Ages, 1913)

May the truth of God uphold us,
the love of Christ enfold us,
and the Spirit's power replenish us,
henceforth and always.

(Collected by P.J. Fisher)

O Christ our only Saviour:
so dwell within us that,
going forth with the light of hope in our eyes,
your word on our tongues,
and your love in our hearts,
we may ever do the will of our heavenly Father.

[S.M.]

O Sun of Righteousness, Light Eternal,
give gladness to all things;
Shine upon us now and ever...
that we may be glad and cheerful in all our dealings.

[S.M.]

Grant unto us, day by day, we pray:
the joy of true living....
that we who seek your service might find your peace.
(Collected by Godfrey Pain)

Set free, O Lord, the souls of Thy servants
from all restlessness and anxiety.
Give us that peace and power
which flow from Thee.
Keep us in all perplexity and distress,
that upheld by Thy strength and stayed
on the rock of Thy faithfulness,
we may abide in Thee now and evermore.
(A Chain of Prayer Across the Ages, 1913)

To Jesus Christ who is the faithful Witness,
the first-born of the dead,
the ruler of the kings of the Earth,
be the glory and the dominion for ever and ever.
(W.M.)

Look graciously upon us, O Holy Spirit:
and give us for our hallowing,
thoughts that pass into prayer,
prayers that pass into love, and
love that passes into life with you for ever.
(Eric Milner-White, 1884-1964)

May God kindle in us
the flame of His indwelling presence –
that our lives may shine as stars
in the clear night sky. *(W.M.)*

Be Thou a bright flame before us;
a guiding star above us;
a smooth path below us;
a kindly shepherd behind us -
To-day, and for ever. Amen. *(Source Unknown)*

May Thy divine power protect and provide for you.
May Thy peace comfort you;
May Thy pardon reassure you,
and Thy precious death redeem you.
May Thy prosperity attend you.
May daily progress be yours along the Heavenly way.

(A Chain of Prayer Across the Ages, adapted)

Enrich, Lord, heart, mouth, hands in me,
With faith, with hope, with charity:
That I may run, rise, rest with Thee.

Amen.

(George Herbert, 1593 - 1632)

May the grace of courage, spontaneity,
and the quiet mind, with all such blessedness
as belongs to the children of
the Father in Heaven, be ours;
to the praise of one God,
world without end. Amen

(Collected by Godfrey Pain, 1934)

The Lord shed forth upon you
showers of Heavenly blessing,
and by his Holy Spirit pour into your hearts
the gift of His own charity.

(Book of Congregational Worship, 1920)

God, I beseech Thee,
guard my soul; sustain my body;
exalt my senses; direct my courses;
regulate my manners; bless my undertakings;
fulfil my petitions;
inspire me with holy thoughts.

Amen

(Lancelot Andrewes, 1555-1626)

From the rising of the sun
to the going down of the same,
of your goodness give us,
with your love inspire us,
by your Spirit guide us,
by your power protect us,
and in your mercy receive us,
now and ever.

*(A Prayer based on the
annual Armistice Remembrance)*

May the Lord lead us when we go,
and keep us when we sleep,
and talk to us when we wake -
for your love's sake.

(A Chain of Prayer Across the Ages)

May God, the Fountain of all blessing,
fill us with the understanding of sacred knowledge.
May He keep us sound in faith,
steadfast in hope,
and persevering in patient charity, always.

(A Collect dating from as long ago as 440AD

May the Lord Jesus Christ fill us with spiritual joy;
May his Spirit make us strong and tranquil
in the truths of his promises.
And may the blessing of the Lord come on us abundantly.

(A Chain of Prayer Across the Ages, 1913)

May you be kept in the love of God,
strengthened by his might,
and garrisoned by his peace, now and evermore.

(Used and Broadcast, World War II)

God Almighty bless us with his Holy Spirit.
Guard us in our going out and coming in.
Keep us ever steadfast in his faith,
free from sin and safe from danger.
(adaptation of Psalm 121)

May the Lord Jesus Christ himself
who is the Light of God,
the Life of Men :
Guide, govern and preserve us
throughout the hours of this new day.
(H.F. Mathews, early 1960s)

In the light of the Lord we go to our work ;
In the strength of the Lord we will live this day;
In the service of the Lord may our lives be spent ;
And may his great will be done.
(H.F. Matthews, early 1960s)

May Jesus our Lord, whose presence brought peace and
joy and love and light, shine into our hearts with
the brightness of His glory, today and for ever.
Amen.
(H.F. Matthews, early 1960s)

Preserve us O Lord while waking
and guard us while sleeping
That awake we may watch with Christ,
And asleep we may rest in peace.
(Book of Common Prayer)

Be present, O merciful God,
and protect us through the silent hours of this night,
so that we who are wearied by the changes
and chances of this fleeting world,
may repose upon Thy eternal changelessness;
through Jesus Christ our Lord.

(Book of Common Prayer)

Abide with us, O Good Lord, through the night:
guarding, keeping, guiding, sustaining, sanctifying,
and with Thy love gladdening us, that in Thee
we may ever live, and in Thee may die,
through Jesus Christ our Lord. Amen

(Archbishop Benson, 1829)

Bless us, O God the Father,
who hast created us;
Bless us, O God the Son,
who hast redeemed us;
Bless us, O God the Holy Ghost,
who sanctifieth us.
O Blessed Trinity, keep us in body,
soul, and spirit
unto everlasting life. Amen

(Weimarischer Gesangbuch, 1873)

O Lord, support us all the day long of this troublous
life, until the shades lengthen, and evening comes,
and the busy world is hushed, the fever of life is over,
and our work is done. Then Lord, in Thy mercy, grant us
safe lodging, a holy rest, and peace at the last;
through Jesus Christ our Lord. Amen

(Source unknown – but sometimes
attributed C.19th to Cardinal Newman)

NEW PETITIONS
FOR MORE TIME

Delay the moment, we pray,
when we must forsake the mountain-top
for barren plain and darkened valley.

Delay, we pray, the occasion of our Communion with Thee
until we have found communion with each other.

I pray the delay of this long journey
that I might say a proper goodbye
to all those I must leave behind.

O God: delay this new task -
this new and awesome responsibility -
for which I know, you know,
I am so dreadfully unprepared.

I would that there be delay within this gloomy tunnel -
that I emerge not into broad daylight :
because it is by struggle not in ease
that I discover my great weakness, your great strength.

Delay our every measure; delay our every treasure;
Delay our pacification, our instant gratification ;
Delay the fulfilment of ambition - sane or vain....
Until we have sought more diligently your direction.

This petition is delayed;
This supplication is delayed;
This intercession is delayed;
Even this confession is delayed ...
      until I can gather up my thoughts;
      until I can find the right words;
      until I can clear my mind of all distractions;
      until I learn to pray.
Lord, teach me to pray.

Delay we pray the last verse of this last hymn;
Delay we pray the last glance of this last meeting;
Delay we pray the last chord of this last overture;
Delay we pray the last word of this last lesson;
Delay we pray the last comfort of this last blessing;
Delay we pray the last breath of this last disciple.

Leader:	We pray for more time
Response:	More time together
Leader:	We pray for more knowledge
Response:	More knowledge of our God
Leader:	We pray for more hope
Response:	More hope for this World
Leader:	We pray for more love
Response:	More love of each other
Leader:	We pray for divine delay
Response:	Longer, longer, longer

Where once we sought answers, now we seek questions;
Where once we sought rewards, now we seek incentives;
Where once we sought the immediate, now we seek delay.

A RECESSIONAL BENEDICTION

Leader [L]	Let us now go out from this place:
Congregation [C]	**In God's name.**
L	In God's strength:
C	**Let us now go out.**
L	Seeking harmony …in all we shall speak or do:
C	**Perfect harmony … in all we speak or do.**
L	Let our hearts and minds be pure:
C	**Purity of heart and of mind.**
L	All those who need to work:
C	**Let us work in God's name.**
L	All those who need to rest:
C	**Let us find our perfect rest in God.**
L	All who fear; shall fear no more:
C	**No more shall we be afraid.**
L	In God's name and in God's strength:
C	**We commit ourselves to every task.**
L	To every eventuality:
C	**We commit ourselves.**
L	To every opportunity:
C	**We commit ourselves.**
L	At break of day:
C	**We offer ourselves to God's plan.**
L	When noon turns to afternoon:
C	**We offer ourselves to God's purpose.**
L	At each home-coming:
C	**We offer ourselves to God's fulfilment.**

L	As night falls:
C	**We offer ourselves to God's replenishment.**
L	There shall be no day or night:
C	**When we forget our maker.**
L	No day or night:
C	**When we forget the God who sustains us.**
L	We shall become whole:
C	**Whole in body and in mind.**
L	And we shall become complete :
C	**Complete in the sight of God our maker.**
L	And whatever we speak or do shall become complete:
C	**Complete and acceptable in God's sight.**
L	Let us not hesitate:
C	**To share our many comforts.**
L	Nor halt:
C	**In sharing our many gifts.**
L	Nor stand back:
C	**When God demands that we should lead.**
L	Nor rush forward:
C	**When God demands that we stand back.**
L	So shall our lives resound with God's praise:
C	**Praise to the God who sustains us.**
L	Praising God:
C	**Let us now go out from this place.**
ALL	**Amen.**

THE BENEDICTUS

"The Benedictus" is the name given to Zechariah's famous prayer following the birth and naming of his son: John the Baptist.

Zechariah [sometimes spelt Zacharias] was married to Elizabeth, cousin to Mary, mother of Jesus, whose own famous prayer: "The Magnificat" runs parallel to The Benedictus.

To-day, The Benedictus is spoken in the Free Churches; it is a canticle in the Church of England; and in the Roman Catholic Church, The Benedictus forms part of the Mass - following the Sanctus.

The Benedictus got its name from the Latin for its first words: "Blessed be the Lord".

THE CONTEXT OF THIS PRAYER
Zechariah was steeped in the Jewish faith. His whole life as a priest was in the service of Judaism. Then came the day he was elected to enter the Holy of Holies of the Temple in Jerusalem. There he burned incense while the whole congregation waited in the sanctuary beyond.

Zechariah already knew the importance of the Benediction in Jewish worship: an importance maintained in synagogues throughout the centuries, and still observed today when Benediction is both a publicly and a privately expressed devotion.

Christianity inherits and shares this sacred tradition which states that the Act of Praise should precede the Act of Supplication.

The ancient Jewish Benediction recited the Goodness and the Might of God - in equal measure. Sacrifices were offered in the Temple to offset the sins and shortcomings of believers. Therefore the Benediction was a hallowing, or consecration, of whatever was to be blessed on the altar.

Further, anything associated with the symbolism and the timing of sacrifice needed hallowing.

The greatest Benedictions of the Jewish faith, words known to Zechariah right from his childhood, are wonderfully beautiful and precise expressions both of the presence of God and our dependence on His mercy.

THE BENEDICTUS
Luke Chapter 1 vv. 68-79

Praise be to the Lord, the God of Israel
because he has come and has redeemed his people.
He has raised up a horn of salvation for us
in the house of his servant David
(as he said through his holy prophets of long ago):
salvation from our enemies -
and from the hand of all who hate us :
to show mercy to our fathers
and to remember his holy Covenant,
the oath he swore to our father Abraham -
to rescue us from the hands of our enemies
and to enable us to serve him without fear
in holiness and righteousness
before him all our days.
And you my child will be called a prophet of the Most High;
for you will go on before the Lord
to prepare the way for him,
to give his people the knowledge of salvation
through the forgiveness of their sins,
because of the tender mercy of our God
by whom the rising sun will come to us from Heaven -
to shine on those living in darkness
and in the shadow of death;
to guide our feet into the path of peace.

ഈൠഈൠഈൠഈൠ

EPILOGUE

Robert Francis Kilvert, the 19th Century curate of Diary fame, travelled one day to the great Cathedral at Canterbury.

The choir singing Evensong that day chose the Anthem:
I will lay me down in peace
For it is Thou, Lord, only
That makest me dwell in safety...

This left Kilvert in tears. A Benediction had been transmitted, seamlessly, effortlessly, from Psalmist to Chorister, Chorister to Worshipper.

The true meaning of a Worshipper is someone who is open to the message, whether that message is an alert or a pacification, an invitation or a distraction, a direction or an option.

Turning the Benediction inside out, imagine what it is like if somebody's last words, before car journey, temporary parting, day's work, sleep or death are words of harshness, words of warning, words of unkindness, worst of all: words of curse.

The Malediction leaves the listener or worshipper with a bad, sad, flavour in the mouth and in the heart. Even where preacher or teacher, parent or neighbour, friend or enemy has a difficult message to give, that should have been said long before an audience leaves.

There must be many people with cause - or no conscience - to regret that they sent someone to interview or expedition, bedroom or grave on the wrong note. The Malediction was a hasty attempt at blame or self-justification, brimming over with a strange mixture of bile and self-righteousness - and it hurt. Sometimes it was fully intended to hurt, sometimes not. The effect is the same.

The words have flown. They cannot be retrieved. So, better make it Benediction than Malediction. Then partner, parent, child, circle, crowd, can all rejoice in those other words of the Psalmist: "I was *glad* when they said unto me, let us go...."

Or perhaps I was glad to find a word in season; glad to discover my words struck the right chord; glad that I spoke in soft tone; glad that my comments were *uplifting*.

Especially, I might have been glad somebody was still there who needed consolation; that my well of faith still had waters to draw upon.

Yet when timing and suitability and gentleness and optimism and self-confidence, and belief in God all *fail* – as they are bound sometimes to do – Benediction is still available.

Like all forms of gratitude, Benediction is probably not voiced enough – or emphatically enough.

If this **BOOK OF BENEDICTIONS** helps more people to remember God from Monday to Saturday, and their neighbour from Sunday through to Sunday next, then it will truly have 'leapt from the bookshelf'.

෫ᄋᲔ෫ᄋᲔ෫ᄋᲔ෫ᄋᲔ

OTHER PRAYER BOOKS

There are a great number of books of prayers in print to be found on the Prayer shelf of any religious bookshop or on the Religion shelf of larger secular bookshops.

There are four main types of prayer book:
- Set books for one particular denomination's worship
- Books of set prayers intended for any act of worship
- Compilations of prayers for use publicly or privately
- Books of prayers written by the authors themselves. [These prayers may take the form of meditations]

It would be impossible to mention more than a few, but, leading on from this Book of Benedictions, it could be helpful to peruse:

THE BOOK OF COMMON PRAYER, and its successors

(Anglican)

THE METHODIST WORSHIP BOOK (MPH, 1999)
THE OXFORD BOOK OF PRAYER (OUP, 1985 and since)
THE SPCK BOOK OF CHRISTIAN PRAYER (SPCK, 1995)
THE BOOK OF ONE THOUSAND PRAYERS (Zondervan 2002)
THE LION PRAYER COLLECTION (Lion, 1996)
AN ANTHOLOGY FOR THE CHURCH YEAR (Mayhew, 1998)

and do try to find **DAILY PRAYER** (by E.Milner-White and G.W. Briggs, PELICAN, 1959) in church, or second-hand.

ACKNOWLEDGEMENTS

To Hodder and Stoughton for passages from The International Bible Society's NEW INTERNATIONAL VERSION of the Bible, first published in 1973.

Extracts from The Book of Common Prayer, the rights of which are vested in the Crown, are reproduced by permission of the Crown's Patentee: Cambridge University Press.

To S.P.C.K. for generous permission to use four prayers in the Celtic tradition from THE EDGE OF GLORY by David Adam (SPCK Triangle, 1989).

To S.P.C.K. again for generous permission to use prayers from PRAYING WITH HIGHLAND CHRISTIANS, by G.R.D. McLean (SPCK Triangle, 1988).

To S.P.C.K. for a prayer by Frank Colquhoun contained in his PRAYERS FOR TODAY (Triangle, 1989).

To The CONTINUUM International Publishing Group for permission to use a prayer from PRAYING ROUND THE CLOCK by Richard Harries, Mowbrays, 1983.

To Methodist Publishing House for permission to use Benedictions from: A BOOK OF WORSHIP FOR PRIMARY SCHOOLS by H. F. Mathews, published by Epworth Press, 1963. Copyright: Trustees for Methodist Church Purposes.

To the Dean and Chapter of Coventry Cathedral for permission to use a Benediction used at the consecration of that city's new cathedral after the terrible destruction of World War II.

To Pearson Education for permission to use a prayer by Dean Eric Milner-White, first published in Longman Green's TREASURY OF DEVOTION.

To The British Broadcasting Corporation for help tracking down certain prayers, many of which were first heard by me and many others on The Daily Service (Radio 4 LW).

To numerous churches and chapels for their diligence thinking about and gathering together photocopied worship material. Marked in this book: [W.M.].

ℰᎧᏩℰᎧᏩℰᎧᏩℰᎧᏩ

By the same Author:

Freed for Devotion
A Carer's Book of Prayers
Godfrey H. Holmes

FREED FOR DEVOTION
A Carer's Book of Prayers

Prayers specifically addressing the situations of paid and unpaid carers. Carers, nurses and chaplains will find this a real encouragement. It can be used for personal quiet times; as a means of widening intercessions in church or chapel or as a starting point in praying with others when we feel our own words are either unavailable or inadequate.

ISBN 0 86071 536 1

Available from your local Christian Bookshop or Direct from Moorleys

"I know of many situations where (these) prayers will speak both directly and powerfully. " *Revd. Dr. Peter Forster, Bishop of Chester*

"I found many of the prayers immeasurably moving, and a most poignant reminder of the variety of circumstances in which people find themselves...." *written on behalf of Rt. Revd. Colin Bennetts, Bishop of Coventry*

"(This) book of prayers is a wonderful resource, with its excellent recognition of what it is like to care for young children or very old people. I am sure that (the) book will be of great help to many."
Rt. Revd. John Oliver, Former Bishop of Hereford

(Godfrey Holmes has) "given much thought to the spiritual needs of carers. .... The outcome is a book of prayers that is honest and realistic about what a carer might want to say to God."
Revd. Canon Roger Grey, Chaplain to the Bishop of Gloucester.

"A collection of prayers both for carers and cared-for ... not pressurising the person being cared for and saying thank you for togetherness. Godfrey Holmes writes from experience and this is evident in the refreshing directness of the prayers."
Across the See: [The Diocese of Norwich]

Also from

MOORLEY'S Print & Publishing

23 Park Rd., Ilkeston, Derbys DE7 5DA
Tel/Fax: (0115) 932 0643

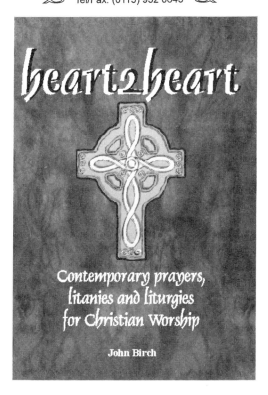

HEART 2 HEART

Contemporary Prayers, Litanies and Liturgies for Christian Worship
by John Birch

This book is an exploration of prayer as well as being a book of
prayer. The prayers cover a wide range of subject matter and draw
on worship in the Early Church, Creation, Seasons,
Healing and Forgiveness, the Cross,
Journeying and Intercessions.

We are growing publishers, adding several new titles to our list each year. We also undertake private publications and commissioned works.

Our range includes:-

Books of Verse:
Devotional Poetry
Recitations for Children
Humorous Monologues

Drama
Bible Plays
Sketches
Christmas, Passiontide,
    Easter and Harvest Plays
Demonstrations

Resource Books
Assembly Material
Songs and Musicals
Children's Addresses
Prayers
Worship and Preaching
Books for Speakers

Activity Books
Quizzes
Puzzles
Painting Books

Church Stationery
Notice Books
Cradle Roll Certificates
Presentation Labels

Associated Lists and Imprints
Cliff College Publishing
Nimbus Press
Headway
Social Workers Christian Fellowship

Please send a stamped addressed envelope (C5 approx 9" x 6") for the current catalogue or consult your local Christian Bookshop who will either stock or be able to obtain Moorleys titles.